A Walk Thru the Book of

PHILIPPIANS

Experience the Joy of the Lord

Walk Thru the Bible

BakerBooks

a division of Baker Publishing Group
Grand Rapids, Michigan

© 2010 by Walk Thru the Bible

Published by Baker Books
a division of Baker Publishing Group
P.O. Box 6287, Grand Rapids, MI 49516-6287
www.bakerbooks.com

Printed in the United States of America

Library of Congress Cataloging-in-Publication Data
    A walk thru the book of Philippians : experience the joy of the Lord / Walk
Thru the Bible.
       p.   cm.
    Includes bibliographical references (p.   ).
    ISBN 978-0-8010-7177-5 (pbk.)
    1. Bible. N.T. Philippians—Textbooks. I. Walk Thru the Bible (Educational
ministry)
    BS2705.55.W35 2010
    227'.607—dc22   2009046940

10   11   12   13   14   15   16   7   6   5   4   3   2   1

Contents

Introduction

Considering his background, he was doing pretty well, but Mark's parents were wondering how long it would take his old habits to die. It had been a year since they adopted him. Hadn't the love they showered on him, the structure they carefully established, and the compassion they poured into him erased his earlier instincts? No, apparently not. He still showed far more signs of his former life than they had expected.

Mark had spent his first five years in a hopelessly dysfunctional family, and it showed. He still acted as though he needed to protect himself, to guard his interests carefully in case no one else did. In spite of all the unconditional love his new family had shown him, he still behaved like someone trying to prove himself. His defensiveness, a legacy of the abuse he once received, showed up almost every time his parents gently tried to correct him. And he still approached every relationship tentatively, always wary of the friendship of others. Though his new family provided a loving, caring environment, experience had failed to teach him that "loving" and "caring" could be real. He would learn, but it would take a lot of time.

That's true for all of us. Regardless of how we came to believe in Jesus and join his family, our backgrounds affect us. Until we

5

are completely immersed in the gospel and it is deeply ingrained in us—a lifelong process—we have a tendency to fall back into our old perceptions and revert to our old ways. Whatever shaped our past rises up in an attempt to drag us back to where we came from. We have to choose not to let it.

Life in the kingdom of God is like leaving one culture and adopting a new one. There's some degree of culture shock, and the adaptation takes time. Though we press ahead toward a new way of life, the old way—our former worldview, relationship patterns, and habits—frequently reminds us of where we've been and causes us to wonder if we can ever change. We can, and in our better moments we know that. But we need reminders that the kingdom we came into is different than the world we have lived in.

That's essentially what Philippians is: a reminder of what kingdom life is all about. Paul hasn't seen the believers in Philippi in several years, and though they are a relatively problem-free church, they are letting old ways seep back into their fellowship. So the apostle reminds them of the selflessness they once learned from Jesus and practiced toward each other, and he calls to mind the joy that was once so familiar to them. They are citizens of another kingdom now, he tells them. The culture of that kingdom is different than the culture of the world around them. They have to consciously choose which culture to embrace.

So do we. That's why Philippians is still a relevant letter and why it has been so helpful to Christians today. It overflows with joy—ideally, that's the mood of the kingdom culture—and it is filled with practical advice about how to think and whom to follow as examples. Immersing ourselves in it can have the same effects that a loving adoptive family can have on a child with a dysfunctional past. It reminds us of who we are, how much we are loved, and what it means to live as children in a new environment.

Philippi

In 42 BC, during the civil war that followed Julius Caesar's death, Roman forces under Mark Antony and Octavian (the future Caesar Augustus) met rival Roman forces under Brutus and Cassius, Caesar's assassins, at Philippi. Octavian and Antony won the battle, and after he became Caesar, Octavian commemorated the victory by declaring the city a Roman colony. As a result, Philippi became heavily Romanized by the first century AD. It was a retirement community for Roman soldiers, had tax-exempt status, was under Roman law, was a center for the emperor cult, and adopted Latin as its dominant language. Though any city of its size would have a diverse population, Philippi's seemed less so. It had a lower concentration of easterners, like Jews, than many other cities in the empire. As small minorities, Jews and Christians in Philippi probably faced quite a bit of opposition and learned to live with it.

Philippi was the first European city Paul and his companions spent time in. Paul meant for his second missionary journey to be a return to churches he had founded on the first journey and a continuing advance into other parts of Asia Minor. But "the Spirit of Jesus would not allow them" to go where they wanted to go (Acts 16:7), and they found themselves directionless until God gave Paul a vision of a Macedonian man crying out for help. So the team crossed the Aegean into Macedonia, and a new frontier for Paul's mission was opened.

That was, according to most historians, in the AD late 40s. Paul passed through the city a few years later on his way back to Jerusalem, but no other contact with the church is mentioned in Acts. We know from his letters that he kept in touch with the Macedonian churches, including Philippi, through reports from coworkers who had been there or who had received news from the Philippians. But there's no evidence that Paul spent substantial time in Philippi after he established the church there. He remembered the fellowship fondly, but he spent most of his time either starting new churches or cultivating the ones that had the most severe problems. The Philippians didn't fit the first category and, much to Paul's relief, seemed to remain outside the other as well.

The Letter

Paul encountered trouble on his last recorded trip to Jerusalem. He became the focus of a riot at the temple and was then bounced around between governors Felix and Festus and king Agrippa. After spending two years under arrest in Caesarea without the charges being resolved, Paul appealed to Caesar and was sent to Rome, where he spent another two years (at least) under house arrest. It was during this time that Paul most likely wrote to the Philippians. He had considerable freedom to receive visitors and outside aid, and the Philippians had sent one of their members, Epaphroditus, to him with both financial and moral support. Paul wrote the letter to thank them and, it seems, to address some of the church's issues that Epaphroditus must have informed him about. The letter is therefore a combination of appreciation for the Philippians' friendship, gratitude for their gifts, and instruction on some of their problems and concerns.

How to Use This Guide

The discussion guides in this series are intended to create a link between past and present, between the cultural and historical context of the Bible and real life as we experience it today. By putting ourselves as closely into biblical situations as possible, we can begin to understand how God interacted with his people in the past and, therefore, how he interacts with us today. The information in this book makes ancient Scripture relevant to twenty-first-century life as God means for us to live it.

The questions in this book are geared to do what a discussion guide should do: provoke discussion. You won't see obvious "right" answers to most of these questions. That's because biblical characters had to wrestle with deep spiritual issues and didn't have easy, black-and-white answers handed to them. They discovered God's will as he led them and revealed himself to them—the same process we go through today, though we have the added help of their experiences to inform us. Biblical characters experienced God in complex situations, and so do we. By portraying those situations realistically, we learn how to apply the Bible to our own lives. One of the best ways to do that is through in-depth discussion with other believers.

The discussion questions within each session are designed to elicit every participant's input, regardless of his or her level of preparation. Obviously, the more group members prepare by reading the biblical text and the background information in the study guide, the more they will get out of it. But even in busy weeks that afford no preparation time, everyone will be able to participate in a meaningful way.

The discussion questions also allow your group quite a bit of latitude. Some groups prefer to briefly discuss the questions in order to cover as many as possible, while others focus only on one or two of them in order to have more in-depth conversations. Since this study is designed for flexibility, feel free to adapt it according to the personality and needs of your group.

Each session ends with a hypothetical situation that relates to the passage of the week. Discussion questions are provided, but group members may also want to consider role-playing the scenario or setting up a two-team debate over one or two of the questions. These exercises often cultivate insights that wouldn't come out of a typical discussion.

Regardless of how you use this material, the biblical text will always be the ultimate authority. Your discussions may take you to many places and cover many issues, but they will have the greatest impact when they begin and end with God's Word itself. And never forget that the Spirit who inspired the Word is in on the discussion too. May he guide it—and you— wherever he wishes.

New Territory

ACTS 16

It had been an eventful twenty-four hours for the *duoviri*. The two magistrates, the city officials who presided over this Roman colony of Philippi, had been much busier than usual. First, there was yesterday's mob scene in the forum, which came dangerously close to getting out of hand. Such incivility has to be handled quickly and decisively, especially in a colony of Rome. So though it was messy business, the two Jews at the center of it were thoroughly beaten and thrown in prison for the night. That seemed to settle the mob down quickly enough, and one could only hope it would remain an isolated incident, well concealed from more powerful magistrates in Rome.

But then there was last night's earthquake—the strongest one in years. What were the gods thinking? Perhaps the slave girl had been right about the Jews serving the Most High God. Could Zeus really be angry enough to shake the whole city like that? Or maybe the Jewish God had actually been awakened by yesterday's business at the forum—though surely he was too far away to care. Regardless, someone up there seemed to notice. Better to be safe than sorry.

That was the conclusion the *duoviri* came to early in the morning, so they hastened the release of the prisoners. They were going to expel the two Jews from town today anyway—the night in prison had just been an object lesson for any other foreigners in the city—so there was no need to keep them confined. But the officers sent to the jail to officially release them came back with an alarming message. The prisoners were actually Roman citizens. Jewish Romans? Roman Jews? Highly irregular. Who could have known? But now the earthquake made perfect sense. Someone *was* angry. And if Rome found out—well, at least two careers would meet their premature demise. Quite possibly the whole city could lose its Roman privileges on such a technicality.

This was serious legal trouble, and the two Jews weren't making it easy. They wouldn't leave town quietly. The magistrates pleaded with them to leave, but they only agreed to do so after spending some time with their friends. Finally, they went on their way. And one could only hope they would be forever discreet about the reason they had to leave.

The arrest, beating, and imprisonment of Paul and Silas was made possible by the city's sense of Roman pride and its disdain for eastern foreigners, especially Jews. But that sense of pride took a huge fall when the Roman citizenship of Paul and Silas was revealed. It was illegal to imprison a Roman citizen without due process, and it was an even bigger violation of the law to beat one. The rods were reserved for second-class subjects—slaves, foreigners, low-status riffraff, and the like. But, curiously, these full-fledged Romans didn't buy into the city's civic pride

THE PYTHON SPIRIT

The slave girl in Philippi had a *pneuma pythona*—a "python spirit"—a powerful spirit of prophecy that used its hosts like a ventriloquist. The python spirit derived its name from the serpent in Greek mythology that empowered the oracle at Delphi and was killed by the god Apollo. This kind of spirit was seen by pagans as being extremely helpful and by Jews and Christians as being demonic and evil. People with a spirit of divination were sometimes known as "belly-talkers" who spoke their prophecies in an altered or unknown voice. While pagan exorcists would perform an exorcism with rituals involving unintelligible chants and animal blood and organs, Paul simply commanded the spirit to leave in the name of Jesus.

up front. They played the part of humble noncitizens until after their harsh treatment. The whole affair could have become a blight on the city's record.

That episode in Paul's ministry highlights several important facts about Philippi: its close ties with Rome, the value it placed on citizenship, its contempt for non-Roman religions like Judaism and, eventually, Christianity. Oblique references to this community's culture will show up later when Paul writes a letter to the Philippian church. The Christians in Philippi will face opposition, yet Paul will encourage them to remain humble and remember their true citizenship. He will use words reminding them of how he behaved when he was in their city and encouraging them to follow his example.

Humble Beginnings: Acts 16:6–15

Paul's experience in Philippi begins with a dramatic dream—a vision of a Macedonian calling him and his coworkers (Silas,

Luke, and Timothy) across the waters. It isn't the direction the missionaries had wanted to go in, but they comply for obvious reasons. God has called.

So they enter Philippi—a "leading city" of Macedonia, Luke tells us—and cannot find a synagogue. The paganism here is more rampant, more openly displayed, than any city in which they have previously ministered. Apparently there aren't enough Jews in this town; a minimum of ten Torah-observant men are required in order to form a proper synagogue. The closest they can find is a gathering of women who worship the God of Israel every Sabbath by the river. Teaching them would ordinarily stretch a Jewish man's sense of propriety, but these are no ordinary Jewish men. One of the women, a Gentile God-fearer named Lydia, is intrigued with the message and believes. A woman of means—she sells expensive cloth and has a home large enough to host all four men—she invites them to stay with her.

Discuss

- Philippi was a place of unexpected ministry. Paul and his companions had not planned to go there in the first place, and then they supposed they would first preach to a synagogue full of Jewish men rather than a riverside gathering of both Jewish and Gentile women. In what ways have you found God's opportunities to be unpredictable? In what ways do you expect him to lead you? How open are you to his redirection?

_____

_____

_____

_____

Earth-Shaking Events: Acts 16:16–40

Focus: Acts 16:16–18; 25–34

The girl was speaking the right message, but it was certainly coming from the wrong spirit. In fact, her echoing of the missionaries' words had become the center of attention and was distracting people from a response. So after several days of putting up with it, Paul finally does something about it. He commands the spirit to leave her.

The girl's owners are outraged. Her fortune-telling abilities had been a prime source of income, and now she was just like any other slave girl, good for nothing more than sweeping floors and running errands. Such an attack on their income couldn't be left unaddressed. They drag Paul and Silas into the marketplace and stir up the mob against them. Their economic outrage conveniently transforms into a racial issue; the troublemakers are immigrant Jews and have been proselytizing in the name of a foreign God. And the charges are technically accurate; it *is* against the law to promote cults that are not officially

LUKE'S HOMETOWN?

Luke referred to Philippi as the "leading city" of Macedonia, though it was neither the largest nor most politically influential in the area. It was an important city but not the most significant. The only other city to have its honor similarly called out in Acts is Tarsus—Paul's hometown (21:39)—leading some commentators to speculate that perhaps Luke's remark about Philippi is a subtle indication of pride in his hometown. If Philippi was in fact Luke's home, it helps explain why his "we" stories in Acts give way to third-person pronouns when Paul leaves Philippi. Luke stayed behind because he had a personal connection with the city.

recognized by the government. With anti-Jewish sentiment stirred up against them, the magistrates take the easy route and appease the crowd. They strip Paul and Silas—Luke and Timothy either weren't there or were spared because of their Gentile backgrounds—and have them beaten Roman-style: with potentially bone-crushing rods.

In a dark, inner cell and with feet in stocks designed to both secure a prisoner and torture him, Paul and Silas begin singing hymns in the middle of the night. Their praises are interrupted by an earthquake violent enough to loosen chains and open doors. The jailer knows the repercussions for losing prisoners, and suicide is preferable. But Paul shouts before he can hurt himself, assuring him that no one has escaped. The praises, the earthquake, and the men who did not flee have convinced the jailer that a powerful deity is at work. What can he do to be saved? Paul and Silas are glad to tell him, and he and his family become believers.

Discuss

- In remarkable foreshadowing of the words he will one day write to the Philippians, Paul exhibits joy in extremely uncomfortable circumstances. What do you think the other prisoners thought of him and Silas? Why do you think they were focused on praying and praising God in spite of their aching, bleeding bodies?

  _____
  _____
  _____
  _____

- Why do you think Paul and Silas didn't see the earthquake and crumbling prison as a God-given opportunity to escape? How would you have interpreted an earthquake that broke your chains? In what ways did God honor their concern for the jailer?

_____

_____

_____

_____

A CASE STUDY

Imagine: You had no idea it was illegal to talk about your faith in Tyrannistan, but your cab driver apparently knows the law quite well. Now your four days and three nights have turned into an undefined stay at the local jail. The officers seemed to enjoy arresting you and cracked a joke about how the prison food will sentence you to death before the judge does. And while you're pretty sure the "death sentence" remark was in jest, the conditions are horrid and the food is as bad as they said. And there's no indication of when they might let you out.

- Which best describes your most likely reaction: outrage and loud demands to call your embassy; fear and an overwhelming urge to curl up in the corner and cry; or trust that God is in control and praise for whatever he's about to do?

- Do you think Paul and Silas experienced any outrage or fear in the Philippian jail before they settled down and worshiped? Why or why not? Do you think there's a relationship between their worship and the deliverance that came? If so, what?

- How can we become the kind of believer who trusts God implicitly in otherwise frightening situations?

Reconnections

PHILIPPIANS 1:1–26

It doesn't seem to matter that the events happened long ago and the footage is obviously decades old. John Rendall and Ace Berg's reunion with Christian the Lion—a YouTube phenomenon that has touched millions—captures a timeless message about the lasting nature of genuine affection and friendship. The two men had seen the lion cub's cramped conditions at Harrods department store in London in 1969 and bought him. But before long, the cub had grown much too large to keep in their apartment. They found a way to return him to Africa, where he could be trained to live in the wild. After a year, John and Ace went to Kenya to visit Christian, but a year in the wild can change an animal. Would he recognize them? Probably not, they were told. Would he be dangerous now that he was more fully grown? Not likely, but one never knows. Finally, Christian's pride was located and the men stood on a hillside to meet him. Christian moved toward them, at first tentatively, and then, in a moment of recognition, quickly. He jumped on them—playfully, affectionately, exuberantly. Yes, he recognized them. Their bonds of friendship were not forgotten.

Real bonds of friendship never are. Any remembrances, any thoughts of a possible reunion after a long absence, cause the past joys and affections of a relationship to resurface. That's the tone of Paul's letter as it opens. He swells with warm memories of his friends. By most estimates it has been at least six or seven years since he has seen the Philippians and well over a decade since he has spent any significant time with them. But he remembers them fondly.

The Christian life is primarily about relationships. We need to remember that. It's easy to get caught up in questions of truth and doctrine, in discussions that turn into arguments about who is right or wrong about issues and practices of our faith. And while learning and defending truth are vital—plenty of Paul's

THE PRAETORIUM

The "palace guard" Paul refers to is the *praetorium*, a word indicating a military headquarters in a center of government. In Rome, thousands of soldiers would have been in this palace guard. Their primary responsibility would be to serve as a human fortress around the emperor and government institutions, and prisoners' guards would be drawn from this contingent. Because Philippi was a Roman colony, many of its young men may have been enlisted to serve in the *praetorium* in Rome. If so, Paul's readers would have had a particular interest in the gospel spreading throughout the guard.

letters are aimed at such purposes—the gospel is always lived in the context of relationships. As Paul wrote in another letter, "If I have the gift of prophecy and can fathom all mysteries and all knowledge, and if I have a faith that can move mountains, but have not love, I am nothing" (1 Cor. 13:2). In his letter to the Philippians, Paul overflows with love. In our relationships, so must we.

A Deep Affection: Philippians 1:1–11

The letter to Philippi is, in the best sense of the term, an emotional appeal. Paul wastes no time getting to the language of feelings—*feel*, *heart*, *long* (or *yearn*), and *affection* are all packed into two verses (1:7–8)—and he continues to use an abundance of emotive terms throughout the letter. He makes it plain that he fully intends to touch his readers' hearts.

Even in the obligatory thanksgiving and prayer—conventional salutations in letters of the time—Paul makes major theological statements. For one thing, God doesn't abandon his pet projects but completes whatever he starts (1:6). This is a comforting thought for anyone in Philippi (or now) who might think God's work in their life is falling apart. When God begins an endeavor, he can see the end of it. So why would he start what he has no intention of finishing? The truth is that he wouldn't. If he began a work of salvation or any other grace in the life of an individual or a church, we have every right to expect him to continue. The fact that he started a masterpiece in us constitutes his commitment to finish it.

Not only does Paul have a deep affection for the Philippian church; he believes he longs for them with Jesus's affection (1:8). Many Christians believe Jesus's love is obligatory—a formal act of his will that comes with being the Savior, as though love is part of his job description. Paul says otherwise. Jesus loves because he wants to, because he finds pleasure in his people. Jesus's love for the Philippians is flowing through Paul, and that love is a joy. It's warm and tender, as Paul will continue to make clear in his letter.

Discuss

- In what aspects of your life has God begun to work? Have you ever felt that he started something in you that he later decided not to complete? Knowing his nature, how thoroughly do you expect him to do his work in you?

  _____
  _____
  _____
  _____

- Do you perceive God as someone who loves you because he has to or because he wants to? How would your life or attitude change if you were fully convinced that God loves you because he enjoys you?

  _____
  _____
  _____
  _____

A Persistent Advance: Philippians 1:12–18

Many people think Paul's imprisonment is a huge blow to the spread of the gospel. Some lament that fact while others seem to rejoice in it. But the Philippians shouldn't worry, Paul tells them. Years before, they had witnessed God using his and Silas's imprisonment as a platform to impact the city with the truth. Now God is using his imprisonment in Rome to spread the gospel throughout the palace guard (1:13) and, apparently, Caesar's household (4:22). What appears to be a huge setback has actually turned out to be a huge opportunity.

Not everyone sees it that way. Some, sensing the leadership vacuum in the church that Paul's imprisonment has seemed to create, have begun preaching in a way to assert themselves and establish their own ministries. Many who have been born into Christ still know how to selfishly compete for attention. Others preach out of pure motives; their hearts are genuinely set on the gospel's advancement, not their own. Either way, Paul assures the Philippians, Jesus is being preached. Again, he turns a negative into a positive.

Paul is doing more than passing on information about his situation. He is modeling a humble, Christ-centered attitude

HOUSE ARREST

Though Paul refers to being "in chains" (1:13), he is probably speaking metaphorically—much like we say "my hands are tied" in a very nonliteral sense. He is most likely writing during his two years of house arrest in Rome. If so, having appealed to Caesar as a Roman citizen, he would be renting his own quarters and paying his own living expenses while being monitored by at least one Roman soldier at all times. Literally being in chains would be an impractical lifestyle for both the guard and the prisoner for such a long time. But consider how a normally active apostle might feel about being confined inside a single apartment, which had become a burdensome financial obligation, while kingdom work was being carried on in the outside world. He probably wouldn't hesitate to use chains as a metaphor for his frustration.

for his readers. He is in the middle of an extremely difficult situation—the kind that would cause many people to question their calling, to second-guess the decisions that got them into their predicament, and to wonder if they will ever be useful again. The Philippians need to see what it's like to face adversity and consider it an opportunity. They need to know how someone can deal graciously with competitive strife. These themes will come up again in the following verses because this is what the Philippians are dealing with. Paul is showing them how he handles such issues himself.

Discuss

- How often have you noticed God using your crisis situations as opportunities for you to demonstrate his truth and character? What can we do to become more aware of and sensitive to those opportunities? Are you in a crisis right now that he might use for good?

  _____

  _____

  _____

  _____

- Self-focus and self-promotion are strong tendencies in almost all human beings, even after we have accepted Christ. What has to happen in our minds and hearts for that to change? How can we keep the self-centeredness of other people from getting under our skin?

  _____

  _____

  _____

  _____

A Difficult Dilemma: Philippians 1:19–26

Paul isn't sure how his trial will turn out. Normally Rome would not consider his offenses to be capital crimes—or even criminal at all—but emperors have been rather unpredictable toward religious troublemakers in the past. Could Paul's life be nearing its end? It's possible, and in Paul's mind that is not necessarily a bad thing. He has been beaten more times than he can remember and traveled more miles than he can count. His body is tired and sore. Departing to be with Christ would truly be gain at any moment in one's life—it is "far better," Paul assures them—but especially under these conditions.

Even so, Paul is convinced that he will remain. The Philippians are praying for him, for one thing, and for him to continue living would mean the presence of Jesus on earth working mightily in one more active apostle for just a little bit longer. Fruitful labor is hard to pass up.

But the apostle is torn between the two options—living or dying—and he seems to consider it a genuine choice. Does he stay or go? And if he decides to go, what could he do about it? Would he refuse to speak up at his trial, just as Jesus did? Or does his choice come down to the simple conviction that God will grant him whatever he asks in this situation? We don't know, but Paul seems to land on a decision even as he writes: the Philippians need him, he wants to see them again, and fruit will result if he stays.

Discuss

- Do you think most Christians feel the same way Paul did about departing to be with Christ? Why or why not? In what ways does our view of death affect the way we live? The way we view the life and death of others?

_____

_____

_____

_____

A Case Study

Imagine: You've been praying about how God wants you to spend the next few years of your life, and two opportunities have recently come to your attention. Deep in your heart, you sense God giving you a choice between them. You are financially independent, so income isn't an issue. You just want to know what to do with your time. Your options are: (1) accept a difficult assignment at an inner-city mission that will involve long hours, heart-wrenching situations, but a lot of fruitfulness; or (2) because you have been so faithful in the past, take it easy with light ministry and minimal fruit in a gated community that offers plenty of comfort and opportunities for refreshment. There's no reason for guilt if you don't choose the hard way that bears more fruit; God is already pleased with your life's work. And you could certainly use some rest, or at least a less strenuous situation than you're used to. But the inner-city position is still an opportunity to accomplish a lot of good during a season of your life that you'll never get back.

- Which would carry more weight in this situation: your lifelong passion to bear fruit for God's kingdom or your legitimate and understandable need to be refreshed? Which do you think you would choose?

- How well do you think this situation represents Paul's dilemma between remaining in the flesh for the sake of ministry and departing to be with Jesus?
- To this point in your life, how have you balanced your needs for rest, comfort, and personal welfare with the always urgent and persistent opportunities to make sacrifices for the kingdom of God?

A Humble Descent

PHILIPPIANS 1:27–2:18

There were legitimate reasons for the lack of people who had volunteered for mission work in inland China. The work was hard, the language was harder, contagious diseases were rampant, conditions were often filthy, opposition was intense, travel was grueling, and the attrition rate was rising. Few Christians wanted to leave the comforts of nineteenth-century England to face hard labor and possible death in the vast interior of Asia. Most had a hard enough time remaining faithful in London.

That's why England was shocked when seven young men from Cambridge passed up their exceedingly bright career prospects to labor in China. Convinced of the need to spread the gospel among the unevangelized millions who didn't live in Asia's coastal cities, the seven joined Hudson Taylor's China Inland Mission in 1885. Many considered their sacrificial gesture noble but misguided—such a waste of their talents and their fine, expensive education. Few understood why they were throwing away such potential.

But they weren't really throwing anything away; they were investing their lives in vital kingdom work. Sure, they would be subject to disease and persecution, and they were certain to get their hands dirty both literally and figuratively. But this was a more important work, a mission that would have eternal significance. And apparently many people eventually agreed. The lives of the Cambridge Seven were worth emulating. Fifteen years after they arrived in Asia, the China Inland Mission had increased from 163 missionaries to over 800.

The greater a person's sacrifice, the more likely it is to be misunderstood. Normal human nature is to advance and improve, to make a profit, to make sure we get something greater for everything we have to give up. When we willingly move in the opposite direction, observers are baffled. Why would someone with so much settle for so little? What rational person would

THE SONG AND THE SERVANT

If Philippians 2:5–11 is one of the church's earliest hymns, the writer may have based it on Jesus's actions in John 13. That's where Jesus demonstrated his humility by taking off his outer robe, donning the garb of a servant, washing his disciples' feet, and then putting his normal clothes on again. It's a graphic picture of the incarnation—the great descent from the throne of heaven to the lowlands of the earth and back again to glory. In Philippians 2, followers of Jesus are told to take the same trajectory in their lives: life, sacrificial service, death, and then resurrection.

throw away comfort or wealth or a bright future with no apparent payoff? It just doesn't make sense.

There is a payoff, of course, but it's invisible to the eyes of the flesh. We bear eternal fruit from the seeds we sow in this life, and the more costly the sacrifice, the more precious it is in God's eyes. That's the dynamic illustrated by Jesus in the incarnation; he left unimaginable glory in order to inhabit a sinful, sorrowful world. Why? Because we were helpless without him. He humbled himself and made an enormous sacrifice because we needed him to. He was willing to forsake his own comfort and lay his life on the line for others. And that, according to Paul's words in Philippians, is to be the pattern for every one of his followers.

Like-Minded: Philippians 1:27–2:4

The Philippians are being opposed. We don't know by whom or to what degree, only that the situation calls for being united, not being frightened, and behaving in a way that characterizes the gospel. After all, Jesus has given them the privilege not only of believing but also of suffering. The dynamics they saw years earlier in Paul's ministry are still being played out in Philippi. They should respond as he did.

Ultimately, that means living in a humble, unselfish way. Paul actually urges the Philippians in this case to make sure their minds conform to the way they feel. If they feel encouraged and comforted, if they have experienced the tenderness and compassion of the Spirit, the right response is to become like-minded with one another. In spite of any differences they have, their emotional bonds should unite them in one purpose. The only way that can happen is for everyone to become radically other-centered—to consider other agendas above their own.

29

Discuss

- Why do you think Paul refers to suffering for Jesus as though it's a privilege that has been granted? Why don't we normally consider it this way?

  _____

  _____

  _____

  _____

- Why is it hard for us, even as Christians, to sacrifice our interests for the interests of others? Is it always right for us to give in to others? Why or why not?

  _____

  _____

  _____

  _____

Sacrificial: Philippians 2:5–11

These verses may be one of the church's earliest hymns, or Paul may be waxing poetic. Regardless, the rhythmic words are loaded with profound theology. Jesus had all of heaven's glory at his fingertips and left it to become a baby in a stable. He divested himself of divine privilege for a time and lived as any human being can. And in his humanness, he chose the form of a servant, even willingly choosing to suffer a death fit for slaves—the most shameful form of execution known.

This, Paul says, is our model. If the Son of God can leave such heights and humble himself to such depths, we can surely abandon our own pride and self-seeking. And if Jesus is any indication, God responds to such humility with honor. Jesus has been exalted to the highest glories of heaven and is worthy of worship from every living being.

Discuss

- To what degree do you think most Christians reflect the kind of humility Paul is talking about?

  _____

  _____

  _____

  _____

Selfless: Philippians 2:12–18

Because of the example of Jesus's radical humility, the Philippians are to work out their salvation "with fear and trembling"—to live out the grace they have been given with deep humility and grateful awe at how God has saved them. In actuality, his Spirit is working and moving through them and giving them

A LIVING, LIQUID SACRIFICE

Paul refers to his life as a "drink offering" here in Philippians 2:17 and also in 2 Timothy 4:6. Along with a lamb and some grain, Israel's priests were instructed to offer wine—a frequent biblical symbol of joy—on the altar every morning and every evening (Exod. 29:38–42; Num. 28:1–8). Unlike some other of Israel's offerings, from which the priests would eat a portion, the drink offering was completely poured out on the altar. It's an Old Testament picture of Jesus's future ministry and served as a twice-daily reminder of the sacrificial life he would live. Paul says it's also a picture of his own life and the attitude all believers are called to embrace.

life, shaping their wills and equipping them in what they are called to do. They live on sacred ground.

That's why complaining and arguing—terms reminiscent of Israel in the Sinai wilderness—are completely out of place. Christians with a contentious attitude don't stand out from the world. They don't shine in the darkness as God intends (Isa. 42:6–7; Dan. 12:3). The selflessness demonstrated by Jesus, who lay down his life for us, and also by Paul, who is being poured out like a drink offering, is what radically impacts the world. Such other-centeredness brings the culture of God's kingdom into a crooked, sinful environment and causes us to shine.

Discuss

- What impact do you think the church would have on the world if every member was completely, radically selfless? What prevents us from being that way? What can we do in practice to develop and maintain a selfless attitude?

_____

_____

_____

_____

A CASE STUDY

Imagine: God has stretched a tightrope high over Niagara Falls and told you that your life depends on your walking across it. He has given you his absolute guarantee that you will not fall; no harm will come to you unless you refuse to cross. Even though you are fully guaranteed to reach the other side and you don't understand why he doesn't just pick you up and set you there, you still have to go through with the act. So slowly, tentatively, and with a fiercely pounding heart, you start walking. The roar of the waters below you is deafening. The wind blows you off balance several times, almost convincing you of your imminent doom, but you never actually fall. And on the few occasions when you dare to look down at the violent waters hundreds of feet below, you're practically paralyzed with fear. It feels as if you will never reach the other shore. Still, you trust his promise and keep walking. Finally, you reach the end and collapse in the wonder and amazement of what you've just experienced.

- Even though you are thoroughly convinced of God's promise to keep you safe, how dependent on his grace would you be while you're high above the falls? In what ways does your precarious situation—even though he has said it isn't actually precarious—serve to keep you focused on him?

- How likely would you be to use God's guarantee of safety as an opportunity to take aimless steps on the tightrope? Do you think his promise would still hold true if you decided to experiment with reckless, acrobatic stunts? Why or why not?

- How well does this hypothetical situation illustrate the process of working out your salvation with fear and trembling? How does awe over the enormity of our salvation keep us from living carelessly or irresponsibly?

The Magnificent Obsession

PHILIPPIANS 2:19–3:16

Jay's father had set it up perfectly. The family business was in great shape; Jay had been immersed in it practically from infancy and had received the finest education in the field. Now everything was ready for Jay to take over whenever his father decided to retire. There was a lot of pride in this heritage and in the name that came with it. So when Jay announced that he had found his mission in life—and it had nothing to do with the business—his parents erupted in protest.

"How could you betray me like this?" his father accused. "Why would you turn your back on all we've given you?" his mother cried. Clearly, he had wounded them deeply, almost as if he had trampled on their sacred ground. Even though Jay's decision wasn't personally directed against his parents, they were offended. He didn't mean it as a rejection of them. He simply found a passion that was much more worthy of investing his life in.

When we find a passion in life—a newfound faith, a consuming mission, a career or relationship that fits perfectly—we leave a lot behind to pursue it. We find that the things we once thought of as extremely valuable suddenly pale in comparison. When our loyalties shift, so does our definition of what's important. We only value the things that take us in the direction we want to go.

Nearly everyone has experienced that dynamic in some area of life, and it certainly applies to those who leave behind a former way of life to follow Jesus. Our priorities shift as soon as we really see him as Savior. The things that once satisfied us become less appealing, while the faith that never mattered much to us suddenly becomes vital. In a lot of ways—some immediate and others more gradual—we experience a transformation.

Paul wrote to the Philippians of his transformation, and there was nothing mild about it. It was dramatic and comprehensive. All that had once mattered to him no longer did, and the Savior he formerly opposed suddenly became the most important passion—in fact, the *only* important passion—of his life. But this isn't just Paul's passion; it's the norm for any Christian. When we become followers of Jesus, knowing him becomes the only real value in life. It redefines who we are and shapes everything we do.

Supporting Servants: Philippians 2:19–30

Paul hopes to send to the Philippians one of his beloved co-workers, Timothy—who, by the way, in case the Philippians haven't caught the hint, is another rare example of a servant-hearted Christian who is completely committed to the interests of Jesus instead of his own. He will also send Epaphroditus back to them. This messenger, sent to Paul by the Philippians with encouraging words and monetary gifts to help with the apostle's living expenses, had fallen seriously ill. He, too, is an example of selfless servanthood, almost dying in his mission to serve Christ by serving Paul. But now that he is better, he is able to return to Philippi.

Discuss

- Paul makes subtle references in these verses to his sense of isolation ("I have no one else like him"), his frustration ("everyone looks out for his own interests"), and his stress ("so that when you see him again . . . I may have less anxiety"). But his joy and gratitude are far more prominent

A MIXED BLESSING

For someone like Paul, there were enormous benefits in receiving a visitor like Epaphroditus. Paul's prison expenses were significant, and though he never specifically asked the Philippians to support him, they sent generous gifts with their messenger. They also would have sent personal correspondence to encourage him and, perhaps, to ask him questions about dealing with certain issues in their congregation. But many have suggested that Epaphroditus had become a considerable burden while visiting Paul and that this section of Philippians is Paul's polite and affirming way of saying, "Thanks, but he really needs to go back home now." Epaphroditus's sickness would have occupied the time of Timothy and Paul's other companions and distracted them from their ministry. Instead of taking care of Paul's needs, as he intended, Epaphroditus had actually become rather needy. His visit may have been an enormous blessing that came at a significant cost.

than these concerns. Using this passage as an example, how can we distinguish between complaining and genuinely expressing troubling issues? How do we know when we've crossed that line?

_____

_____

_____

_____

Only Jesus: Philippians 3:1–16

A significant percentage of early Christians had come to faith in Jesus from a background of Pharisaism—strict and excruciatingly thorough observance of the Torah, the law of Moses. It's only natural, then, that they would emphasize God's commands to circumcise male children and to keep kosher. After all, these commands were part of God's "everlasting" covenant (Gen. 17:7, 11). And Paul, a Pharisee himself, certainly valued the law of God and continued to observe some temple vows and sacrifices after his salvation (Acts 21:26). But he has also seen the Spirit saving and cleansing Gentiles apart from the law of Moses—by grace through faith alone.

Apparently, some "Judaizers"—those who insist that a Gentile's response to salvation should include strict observance of Torah as the Pharisees interpret it—have been troubling the Philippian church, specifically by insisting on circumcision. They can undoubtedly quote more Scripture and sound more authoritative than the Gentile leadership in Philippi, so their words are not taken lightly. But Paul bluntly calls them "dogs" and evildoers, and refers to his own Jewish pedigree as "rubbish" (literally "manure" or "dung") in comparison with the value of knowing Jesus. His entire identity—the identity of any believer, for that matter—is

UNCLEAN DOGS

Paul uses sharp irony in his words about the Judaizing teachers of early Christianity, both here and in his other letters. In Galatians, he wishes that the mutilators of the flesh (that is, circumcisers) would mutilate (literally, emasculate) themselves. In Philippians 3, he calls them "dogs," a derogatory term often applied to Gentiles. Jewish teachers considered dogs to be unclean, immoral creatures. By using such a strong word Paul is saying those who are trying to make Gentile believers ritually clean are themselves unclean. These are shocking words. Any first-century Jew, even a Christian one, would cringe to hear someone say that "neither circumcision nor uncircumcision has any value" (Gal. 5:6) or to hear someone call his rich Jewish heritage "dung." Paul's harsh treatment of these teachers demonstrates just how dramatically this Pharisee has changed.

tied completely to Christ within him. Nothing can make a believer more righteous than the sacrifice of Jesus and union with him, whether at the moment of salvation or any time afterward. Through the power of a relationship with him, we become like him in his sufferings, in his death, and in his resurrection.

In fact, this is all that matters. The Christian life is, quite simply, a close, intimate connection with Jesus. It's a matter of always growing onward and upward in him, forgetting what lies behind. Any "gospel" that defines righteousness in external terms rather than the Spirit living and working within us is, according to Paul, a step backward. We are to press ahead.

Discuss

- Is there anything from your past or present—family status, education, experience, accomplishments, etc.—that tends to shape your identity more than your relationship with Jesus does? If so, what? How can we become so single-minded about knowing Jesus that we consider all else garbage by comparison?

_____

_____

_____

_____

- We know the gospel allows us to put past mistakes behind us, but Paul insists on putting even his past accomplishments behind him. Are there any "good" things God might want you to leave behind in order to progress with him? If so, what?

_____

_____

_____

_____

A CASE STUDY

Imagine: According to legend and spotty records, a Spanish galleon sank about ten miles off the coast of your hometown. A lifelong diving enthusiast, you spent most of your free time looking for it, but recently your search had taken you well beyond "free time." People warned you about your obsession, but their words went unheeded. You were determined to find the millions of dollars' worth of gold and jewels hiding beneath the waves.

Until a few weeks ago, however, you had only found a few artifacts from less lucrative ships. Sure, some of them were historically important, and you enjoyed both the discovery process and your small contribution to the field of underwater archaeology. The local museum appreciated your finds too. But thanks to a new and unconventional mapping method, your entire world changed when you realized that the elusive Spanish galleon you've been searching for actually sank several miles from where you once thought. And when you finally find it, the treasure is beyond your imagination. It is actually worth billions of dollars, not millions, and you become front-page news the moment your discovery is confirmed. Your life will never be the same.

- How would you respond to local historians who, despite your amazing discovery, insist that you should keep combing the sea floor further up the coast—just in case your recent find was the wrong ship? Or to other treasure hunters who proudly declare that the older, more conventional maps are still being used by most experts?

- Why did Paul's relationship with Jesus make all other concerns irrelevant? Do you think it was possible, in his mind, to have fellowship with Jesus and yet be unsatisfied in other areas of life? Why or why not?

- Being as honest as you know how to be, to what degree do you think you've found full satisfaction in Jesus? How do you think Paul would advise an unsatisfied Christian to continue to seek fulfillment?

Joy

PHILIPPIANS 3:17–4:9

It used to be one of the happiest churches in the region, with a strong spirit of joy permeating the fellowship. Worship services were buoyant, friendships were rich and vibrant, prayer and study groups were thriving, and new members were being drawn in weekly. But somehow, imperceptibly—no one knows when or why it started—church turned into more of an obligation than a privilege. Simple suggestions for the staff evolved into not-so-subtle criticism of how things were done. Mild differences of opinion between members morphed into long-standing friction that divided old friends. People who enthusiastically volunteered for the honor to serve became people who were grudgingly recruited for tasks of service. And worship services that once pulsated with life turned into a stale routine.

It's hard to know exactly what causes the flames of joy to shrink into dull embers, but it happens all the time. A series of setbacks, a few bad moods, some misunderstood comments, a critical attitude—any number of catalysts can steal joy from a congregation and cause its upward and outward focus to turn inward. Before long, the fellowship has gone through an entire climate change, and no one knows why. Sometimes no one is even aware that it has happened—or not until it's too late, anyway. All anyone can tell is that it isn't like it used to be.

That seems to be the case in Philippi. The once-vibrant congregation—which, to be fair, still seems to be fruitful—has lost its joy. Some degree of self-seeking has crept in among its members, some false teaching seems to have made inroads, and some level of friction persists. Toward the end of his letter, Paul addresses issues of disunity, discouragement, and anxiety. Though we apply his words in chapter 4 for individual use—and they are profound truths that certainly do have bearing for our personal lives—his teachings about being anxious for nothing

"TAKE ME, FOR EXAMPLE"

Some readers perceive Paul's instructions to follow his example as arrogance, the exact opposite of the humility he wishes to portray. But in Greco-Roman culture, his words are almost embarrassingly humble at times. Pride was considered a high virtue in Roman society, while humility was seen as a contemptible weakness. So even though ancient writers avoided praising themselves profusely, they still boasted within acceptable norms. Paul falls well short of those norms, declaring outright that he isn't perfect or fully mature (3:12). In fact, his simple pleas for the Philippians to follow his example—implicit earlier in the letter, now explicit in 3:17 and 4:9—are mild for a teacher of his stature.

and focusing on praiseworthy thoughts were originally intended for a group setting. He directed them at a congregation that may well have fallen prey to backbiting, discouragement, and lifeless labor. He sought to restore the joy of their fellowship.

We benefit by his words, both as individuals and as congregations. Most of us have been in group settings that were tense and frustrating. All of us, at one time or another, have personally been anxious or discouraged. The remedy, according to Philippians, is an infusion of joy. As he nears the end of the letter, Paul helps us find it.

A Heart's True Home: Philippians 3:17–4:1

Paul continues to overflow with emotion. He has expressed deep joy and gratitude for Philippian believers, then outrage at the circumcisers, then zeal for knowing Jesus, and now grief over those who are destined for destruction. They are investing their lives in fading, self-centered, earthly kingdoms. On the other hand, our citizenship—that of Paul, the Philippians, and all believers—is in heaven. When Paul appealed to his Roman citizenship years before in Philippi, he was exploiting a political reality. But his feet are really planted in another kingdom that operates under a completely different power. That kingdom—or its King, rather—transforms us and enables us to remain stubbornly, persistently faithful.

Discuss

- What do you think Paul means when he says, "Their mind is on earthly things" (3:19)? In practical terms, what do you think it means to be a citizen of heaven? How does someone live differently when they know that they belong to an unearthly kingdom? How does being a citizen of heaven strengthen us for life in the world?

_____

_____

_____

_____

Climate Change: Philippians 4:2–9

Up to this point, Paul has spoken in general terms of disputes and complaints, but now he names names. Two women in the church, Euodia and Syntyche, are at odds with one another. Both were faithful workers with Paul in the past and probably are still influential leaders. Paul appeals to other leaders in the church to help them reconcile, but instead of telling them simply to be at peace, he tells them to rejoice. Why? Because joy makes a lot of other instructions superfluous. Strife arises out of discontentment, not out of joy. Rejoicing people are much more likely to treat others with gentleness.

Paul seeks to rid the Philippians of anxiety, and his prescription is simple: pray about everything with a spirit of gratitude. Like joy, thankfulness tends to resolve a lot of issues, including anxiety; and it seems to be the right seasoning for every request. One of the Bible's most comforting promises results from such prayers: the peace of God, which transcends all understanding, will guard our hearts and minds in Christ.

Paul urges the Philippians to create a new culture in their fellowship. Instead of being preoccupied with offenses, disputes, false teachings, and other such negative thoughts, they should focus all their attention on whatever is true, noble, right, pure, lovely, admirable, excellent, and praiseworthy. A mind filled with such beauty and truth has little room for pettiness, and a church in that climate has little room for friction.

Discuss

- Do you think it's possible to change the climate of a congregation with Paul's instructions in 4:4–9? Why or why not? What about the climate of your personal life? What part do we play in this change? What part does God play?

  _____

  _____

  _____

  _____

THE LOYAL YOKEFELLOW

In 4:3, Paul appeals to his "loyal yokefellow"—or "true companion," in some translations— to help Euodia and Syntyche resolve their dispute. The fact that he can refer to someone without using his or her name implies that this person is a leader in Philippi and perhaps even the primary addressee of the letter. But who is it? Some have speculated that the reference is to Luke, who often worked closely with Paul and seems to have remained in Philippi when Paul left. (This is based on Luke's transition in Acts 16 from using the inclusive "we" to third-person pronouns after Paul departed the city.) Others have suggested that the true companion is Lydia, Paul's first convert in Philippi, but who is not mentioned outside of Acts 16. In fact, the word *companion* is sometimes used in other places to mean "wife," fueling far-fetched speculation that Paul and Lydia got married at some point during his ministry—presumably after he had written 1 Corinthians 7:8–9. Regardless of who this person was, it's clear that Paul still had a close personal contact in the Philippian congregation and that he trusted him or her to be a peacemaker without Paul having to take sides.

A Case Study

Imagine: You've been battling discouragement a lot lately. Some of your friends worry that you might be depressed and suggest you should see a counselor. You aren't sure whether your discouragement is entirely due to some adverse circumstances—and admittedly, things haven't been going all that well for you—or due to some long-standing negative thought patterns you need to break out of. It's probably some of both. Regardless, you have a hard time staying positive.

- How effective would it be for a Christian friend or family member to tell you to rejoice in spite of your circumstances? How effective would it be to read the same instruction from Paul's hand (4:4)? To what degree is joy a choice? If you don't have it, how can you get it?
- Do you think Paul's instructions to rejoice and not be anxious are realistic? Why or why not?
- What role does the community of believers play in cultivating joy among its members? What role can you play in contributing to a climate of joy?

Gifts and Gratitude

PHILIPPIANS 4:10–23

The church's leaders were gratified by the overwhelming response to their appeal. They spelled out to the congregation exactly what would be needed to complete the building campaign, and the checks started pouring in. Finally, when the project was complete and it came time to recognize donors for their generosity, a special ceremony was held.

For the celebration, the church printed a commemorative booklet that listed each donor by name. The first section listed those who gave purely out of a sense of obligation. Several pages were needed for that. Then came the names of those who had given because they wanted some say-so over how the new building would be used in the future. The next section listed in big, bold letters those who had donated because they wanted recognition for their gifts. Then came a smaller section of people who had given because they felt sympathy both for the staff who had to make such humiliating appeals for money and for the people who really needed new building space. And finally came the list of those who gave out of a love for God and a desire to partner with him in his mission.

Absurd? Of course. We only know monetary gifts by dollar amount and the name of the giver. All of the motives behind people's generosity are invisible to us. But they are an open book to God, and he reads them carefully. Most of our works and gifts come out of a combination of motives. Even those who give primarily because they love God and want to partner with him in his work may be slightly offended if they aren't thanked or recognized; and even those who give primarily out of a sense of obligation may truly want their resources to be used by God because they love him. God gives us grace for our mixed intentions. But ideally, we know what kind of gifts he prefers: those that flow out of a heart that loves him and wants to offer him the very best it can offer. Those are the purest sacrifices that please him.

MACEDONIAN GENEROSITY

Paul wrote in 2 Corinthians 8:1–2 that the Macedonian churches, of which Philippi was one, gave generously out of their "extreme poverty." That makes their gift to Paul all the more meaningful, but it also perhaps explains what Paul meant in 4:19 by God supplying all their needs. Though we often over-spiritualize New Testament promises like this one—and God's provision certainly does apply to spiritual blessings—the Philippians needed basic material provision. Verses like Deuteronomy 15:10, Psalm 37:25–26, and Proverbs 19:17, all of which affirm God's tangible resources for those who are faithful and generous, would have undoubtedly shaped Paul's perspective.

In the kingdom of God, motives are a big deal. That's one reason Paul is so appreciative of the Philippians' gifts to him; he knows what kind of heart those gifts came from. They were an expression of the Philippians' love and their desire to partner with him in his work. More than that, they were an offering to God.

It's a good idea in any Christian activity—giving, serving, fellowshiping, etc.—to examine our motives frequently. If we don't, we may find ourselves serving God out of obligation and guilt rather than gratitude, or trying to promote ourselves among his people rather than simply relating to them in love. God declared long ago that he looks at the heart. We do well to look at it too.

Always Content: Philippians 4:10–13

Years earlier, the Philippians had sent Paul monetary support "again and again" while he was in Thessalonica (4:16). So when he speaks of their "renewed" concern, he is remembering their long history of generosity. He is careful to clarify—perhaps for the sake of any newcomers when this letter is read in the congregation—that he never asked for financial gifts and could get along fine without them. He has, after all, been in circumstances of extreme need and learned to be content in the midst of them. He has also learned how to manage abundance with spiritual maturity—perhaps a harder task to handle gracefully. He can get by in any situation because God gives him strength.

Discuss

- Contentment is elusive, especially when we feel that we're missing out on something we need or want. What was

Paul's "secret"? How did he maintain his sense of contentment? What can we do, in practical terms, to adopt his attitude if we don't already have it?

_____

_____

_____

_____

Always Supplied: Philippians 4:14–23

Greco-Roman gift giving is a complicated thing involving status and reciprocity. If Paul simply thanks the Philippians for their gift, he may be making a statement about his future obligations to them or implying an unequal relationship of patronage between him and the church. So he writes carefully in the language of equality, as he has done from the beginning: they are partners in the gospel (1:5) and have shared in God's grace with him (1:7), and again they "share" in his troubles (4:14) and "in the matter of giving and receiving" (4:15). Repeatedly Paul affirms

GOD'S GIFT-GIVING ETIQUETTE

In Greco-Roman culture, receiving a gift generally obligated the recipient to repay it in a way proportional to his means, either monetarily or through some favor or act of service. But Paul is not in a position to repay the Philippians, and in light of his past efforts on their behalf he may not feel a need to repay them. He therefore reframes the normal social expectation: the Philippians have given primarily to God, not to Paul. Their generosity is an offering, an acceptable sacrifice. So the responsibility to reciprocate shifts from Paul to God himself, who will certainly respond to the church's generosity by meeting their needs out of his abundance.

the joint efforts and common mission between God, himself, and the believers of Philippi. They are not only co-laborers; they are bound together in friendship. And because of their generosity toward him—but really toward God—their needs will be fully met by God's glorious provision in Christ.

Discuss

- It has been said that our money always flows in the direction of our loves—or, in other words, that our pocketbooks reflect our priorities. To what extent do you think that is true in your life? How well does your spending reflect your love for God?

_____

_____

_____

A CASE STUDY

Imagine: You've always given faithfully to your church—a tithe most of the time, or at least something close to it. The economy turned sour last year, however, and work has been hard to come by. You've been having trouble making ends meet. You recite Philippians 4:19 often, trusting God to meet your every need. But he seems to be stretching your beliefs in that area, or perhaps he's stretching your definition of "need." You know he's faithful, but your hard times make you feel like he isn't keeping his end of the bargain.

- In what ways, if any, does Philippians 4:19 constitute a bargain with God? Do you think the promise of this verse is conditional on our giving? Why or why not?

51

- From what you know of Scripture, does God generally meet only the basic needs of his people, or does he bless his people beyond their needs? Are his blessings earned, freely given, or some of both?
- In what ways have you noticed God respond to your generosity toward him?

Conclusion

The Philippian church began when a team of missionaries met Lydia by the river and "the Lord opened her heart to respond to Paul's message" (Acts 16:14). That description sets the tone for the church's future. It's an open-hearted congregation not only toward God but also toward the apostle who first brought them the gospel. From its first appearance in the pages of the New Testament to its last, the church in Philippi is a vessel for the affection of Christ.

This church began somewhat as a surprise. Philippi wasn't even on Paul's original agenda. But the nice surprise turned out to be a vital source of joy for the apostle and a significant means of financial support. Unlike other churches plagued by immorality (Corinth) and false teaching (Galatia), the Philippians were relatively problem free. Other than some discouragement and internal friction, they were exemplary. That positioned them to be the recipients of one of the least corrective and most encouraging letters in the Bible.

Though the letter is a response to the Philippians' generosity in the gift they sent, it's much more than that. And though the letter contains advice about various issues the church is facing, it's much more than that too. At its highest level, it's an explanation of how God's character becomes ours, how our passion for Jesus unites us in purpose with each other. When our focus is on Jesus, we lose sight of the things that divide and discourage us. We can face opposition, handle strife, serve selflessly, rejoice always, be content—or as Paul says, "do all things"—through him who strengthens us. Philippians reminds us of that with some of the Bible's most uplifting words. It's a celebration of fellowship with God and with each other—and a free expression of an open heart.

Leader's Notes

Session 2

Philippians 1:19–26, discussion question. The direction this discussion takes may depend somewhat on the participants' stage of life. Some may feel that the question is a little morbid—although that in itself highlights the difference between the early church's view of death, in light of the resurrection of Jesus, and that of many Christians today. Help the group realize that the real focus is not on death itself but on the exceedingly glorious blessings of being with Jesus—and that we are all called, at any stage in life, to invest our hearts not in the here and now but in eternity.

A Case Study. Some people, like Paul, drive themselves hard and spend themselves relentlessly for the kingdom of God. They accomplish a lot but may burn out quickly. Others pace themselves more carefully. They may or may not accomplish as much in as short a time, but they are able to last much longer. There is no biblically right or wrong way to spend oneself for the kingdom, so avoid discussing the issue in those terms. Instead, help participants seek to find the right balance in light of their individual calling and giftedness.

Session 3

Philippians 1:27–2:4, discussion questions. Help participants realize how difficult Paul's instructions are in this section. The situation in Philippi probably involves at least two groups of people, each thinking they are right and the others are wrong. The real question here is whether we give up the "right" point of view and let the "wrong" people have their way. Does Paul (or God) expect us to always sacrifice our convictions for the sake of fellowship? If that question doesn't come up in the course of conversation, bring it up—but be prepared for the possibility that this could develop into a very long discussion.

Philippians 2:12–18, discussion questions. These questions invite your group to imagine what a thoroughly humble, selfless community would be like. How would people treat each other? What legitimate conflicts, if any, might arise? How appealing would this kind of community be to outsiders? The obvious implication is that this is the kind of community Jesus called his disciples to live in (there are snapshots of it in Acts 2:42–47 and 4:32–35) and that these are the attitudes that develop when his Spirit is present and freely working. Most Christians have never experienced a community in which radical humility is the norm, at least not for any great length of time. To whatever degree possible, let participants wrestle with why this is the case. See if your group can come up with some practical ways to develop this kind of community.

A Case Study. This hypothetical situation is obviously absurd on the surface, but it also captures the tension we have between relying fully on God's grace and not taking it for granted. Many Christians have stumbled over Paul's instructions to work out our salvation with fear and trembling, as though we are still earning some portion of our deliverance from sin. But that would so thoroughly contradict Paul's beliefs as he has stated them in other letters that this can't be his meaning. It's much more likely that he is encouraging believers to remember the enormous gap between their sin and God's righteousness, as well as the amazing work Jesus did to bridge that gap. That produces awe, even fear and trembling, and causes us to live out our salvation carefully—much like someone looking down from a high wire at how far he could fall even when he's guaranteed not to.

Session 4

A Case Study. The "right" answer to these questions may seem obvious, but don't let group members pass over them too quickly. The second group of questions in particular raises a difficult topic. Is it possible to know Jesus deeply yet be unsatisfied? The church is full of people who are completely unsatisfied in their work, singles who long to be married, married people who wish they were single, couples who desperately want to have a child, sick people who urgently want to be healed, and so on. Bring up some examples like this if participants don't do so themselves. There is a fundamental level at which Jesus meets our deepest needs right now, but God still allows certain longings and hungers in our lives to go unfulfilled or certain frustrations to go unresolved for a time—sometimes an excruciatingly long time. The tension between these two truths can provoke a fruitful discussion.

Session 5

Philippians 3:17–4:1, discussion questions. To help group members grapple with Paul's contrast between "earthly" and "heavenly" things, try rephrasing the question with specific examples. Does "earthly" refer only to sinful ways? Does "heavenly" rule out the concerns we have on earth such as marriage and family, jobs and income, etc.? Is the difference only a matter of perspective on the issues all human beings face? Or is Paul implying that Christians should withdraw from the world—from politics, economics, and culture, for example—as some throughout history have thought? Even within these broader questions, you may want to bring up specific issues and ask what the difference between an earthly approach and a heavenly approach to those issues would be.

A Case Study. This discussion requires a great deal of sensitivity. The number of people wrestling with discouragement and depression, even within the church, is staggering. Many people are encouraged by the instruction to rejoice as an act of the will, and others are adamant that joy isn't like a switch that can be turned on and off. Be aware of the fact that depression has many causes, both emotional and physiological, but also affirm that the Bible is not unrealistic in what it tells us to do. If possible, guide the conversation into a healthy discussion of what real joy is (and isn't), how finding it can be a daily spiritual battle, and how we can be filled with it even in hard times.

Session 6

Second Corinthians 8–9 provides very helpful background for many of the questions in this session. It's Paul's longest recorded discussion on the matter of giving and receiving.

Bibliography

Arnold, Clinton E., ed. *Zondervan Illustrated Bible Backgrounds Commentary.* Grand Rapids: Zondervan, 2002.

Fowl, Stephen E. *Philippians.* Grand Rapids: Eerdmans, 2005.

Kaiser, Walter C., Jr., and Duane Garrett, eds. *Archaeological Study Bible.* Grand Rapids: Zondervan, 2006.

Keener, Craig S. *The IVP Bible Background Commentary: New Testament.* Downers Grove, IL: InterVarsity Press, 1993.

Twelftree, Graham H. *In the Name of Jesus: Exorcism among Early Christians.* Grand Rapids: Baker Academic, 2007.

Witherington, Ben III. *New Testament History: A Narrative Account.* Grand Rapids: Baker Academic, 2001.

Woodroof, Tim. *A Distant Presence: The Story Behind Paul's Letter to the Philippians.* Colorado Springs: NavPress, 2002.

WALK THRU THE BIBLE®

Helping people everywhere
live God's Word

For more than three decades, Walk Thru the Bible has created disciple-
ship materials and cultivated leadership networks that together are
reaching millions of people through live seminars, print publications,
audiovisual curricula, and the Internet. Known for innovative methods
and high-quality resources, we serve the whole body of Christ across
denominational, cultural, and national lines. Through our strong and
cooperative international partnerships, we are strategically positioned to
address the church's greatest need: developing mature, committed, and
spiritually reproducing believers.

Walk Thru the Bible communicates the truths of God's Word in a way
that makes the Bible readily accessible to anyone. We are committed to
developing user-friendly resources that are Bible centered, of excellent
quality, life changing for individuals, and catalytic for churches, ministries,
and movements; and we are committed to maintaining our global reach
through strategic partnerships while adhering to the highest levels of in-
tegrity in all we do.

Walk Thru the Bible partners with the local church worldwide to fulfill
its mission, helping people "walk thru" the Bible with greater clarity and
understanding. Live seminars and small group curricula are taught in over
45 languages by more than 80,000 people in more than 70 countries, and
more than 100 million devotionals have been packaged into daily maga-
zines, books, and other publications that reach over five million people
each year.

Walk Thru the Bible
4201 North Peachtree Road
Atlanta, GA 30341-1207
770-458-9300
www.walkthru.org